Archivum

Archivum

Theresa Muñoz

First published 2025 by
Liverpool University Press
4 Cambridge Street
Liverpool
L69 7ZU

British Library Cataloguing-in-Publication data
A British Library CIP record is available

The manufacturer's authorised representative in the EU for product
safety is:
Easy Access System Europe, Mustamäe tee 50, 10621 Tallinn,
Estonia
https://easproject.com (gpsr.requests@easproject.com)

ISBN 978-1-83624-301-4 softback

Typeset by lexisbooks.com
Printed and bound in Poland by Booksfactory.co.uk

For my dad, Arturo,
all my love

'Each collected object or manuscript is a pre-articulate empty theatre where a thought may surprise itself at the instant of seeing. Where a thought may hear itself see.'

Susan Howe, Spontaneous Particulars:
The Telepathy of Archives

Contents

Prime 1

Special Collections 2

James Gillespie's School for Girls 3

The Prime of Miss Jean Brodie wins the Oscar, 1970 5

Register of Corrected Entries 6

Water of Leith 7

Playfair steps 8

Brothers 9

Muriel Spark's Mum's Letters 10

The Handover 11

Frances 12

Dear Frances 13

Are you happy? 14

Dim Sum Vortex 15

No. 18 16

Foucault 17

Cashino 19

Lines 20

Animals 21

Hôtel Chevillon, Grez-Sur-Loing 22

Fear of future loneliness 23

Kindness 24

Hinterland 25

Summerhall 26

Carry 27

Ordinary life 28

Balmoral Clock 29

White Gloves 30

Your Paris   31
Muriel's Diaries   32
Secrets   33
Footnotes comparing Muriel and I   34
Muriel Spark's Love Recovery Club   35
Couples Therapy   37
Jam   39
Queen Street Gardens   40
Names   41
Meghan and Harry move to Vancouver Island   42
Letter from Marie Battle Singer and James Burns Singer 43
Last Words of Eliza Junor   44
Love in a stone   45
Let's be Elizabeth and Marianne   46
After the Pamphlet   47
Look   48
Ghost   49
Pointillism   50
Holiday   51
Purple   52
On Arthur's Seat   53

Notes   54
Acknowledgements   56

Prime

Be brutal. Be emotionally unavailable.
Be someone who makes the lamb-hearted
flinch. A photo freezes one long
thought, one of a million switch blade moments.
This one of her is seriously lit: uptown lady
swathed in azalea tint, honey backcombed hair
scalloped by life's swift pace.
That spring, a leather beaded vest was a must.
She was forty, it was the sixties: west pouring light
made her look thoughtful, straight as hedgerows.
Surely this was her prime. Her son was grown
& her books newly flung in the world. Now
there was space in each day to consider the end
of pauses, wet curls of leaves poking the kitchen window.
She was alone, her own best companion.
Snarl of *what now* in her eyes.

Special Collections

Inside the reading room it's me
with letters, pink and crinkly, thin as gift wrap.

For months
I scrunch my face
at each one
like a crossword –

the sedative quality of immersion
means no getting up, no water, nothing,
until shadows flood the carpet.

It's a skill, isn't it, reading the letters of others?
No openings
for conversations, no spying
the author's disapproving face.

Only this: picking half-truths
amongst the slanted lines, shuffling papers
into a stack both light and heavy.

Be better, I tell myself. *Be worthy of this journey.*

James Gillespie's School for Girls

This poem is about that clarifying pang
when your tub of school photos
       is your face, at a distance from your face
and what it means, if anything at all

since memory works its cross-purposed way –
our brain's northern garlic cloves
       form our temporal lobe
and without that synaptic alert I wouldn't know

my face in the elevator, rising to archives again,
white-gloved as a cartoon mouse. I rummage
       for the acetate square
with curled edges, varnished as an ice pond

mid-winter. This famous photo:
thirty-eight girls from the school on the links
       Muriel Spark's chubby heart face
skimming pal Frances, fringe in a scissor-cut path,

and the Brodie set who inspired that book,
humble as flowers at the foot of a wall.
       They're all dead now –
including the teacher, Miss Kay in her blue cloche hat,

and some part in me rises and flips, recalling
snow prints on the playing green,
       lining up to line up more, in these memories
we find our own faces easily, like a pin on a map.

Like a bang, when you see your face again.
Like a bang, is my half-formed thought, on the hot bus
       swaying home,
I push my key into the lock, drop my bag on the floor,

because at some point we sail through the door
to adulthood, and since we never learn
        to love ourselves,
we love ourselves, trying to learn.

The Prime of Miss Jean Brodie
wins the Oscar, 1970

'thank you for creating such a wonderful character for me to
     play' –
telegram from Maggie Smith, London 1970

Holding the telegram, I wondered what Maggie Smith
was thinking, as her fame erupted one London evening.

Did her eyes twinkle brown lights
as her character was known for.
Did she wear purple, an avenging shade.
For most of the film I admired her waist.

Who can know if her hair was the same q-tip style,
if she held her nose high in the air or strode out guns blazing,
if she remembered shouting *Assassin!* at Sandy,
a scene not in the book but gave the film a dramatic ending.

Poor Sandy, who slept with the art teacher,
her milk-white body uncoiling from the bed,
an act that seemed unnecessarily provocative.
The dialogue lagged, film's scenery was too mute,
grey walls seemed drab at the school for girls.

Who can know if Maggie wrote to Muriel
in her staged Bruntsfield accent,
or, if after saying STOP on the telegram
she recalled Edinburgh in its prime, its fiery hour,
when the sky over the meadows turns a gritty rose
and the city seems to burst apart –

and if she hated being Jean Brodie, secretly,
since one's prime was also one's downfall.

Register of Corrected Entries

I'm thinking about time. How it distils shelves of records
in covers of mustard. Pine. Autumn is on my mind,
autumn with its breezes of worry. I've spent the morning
in a sweater and watching my own hand turn pages.
Vanilla paper. Longhand neat in boxed columns.
Register of corrected entries for birth, deaths and unions.
A tricky way to say: here is a book of regret.
When a couple divorced, it was added
to a separate register, to not disrupt history.
Absentee fathers had their names added
afterwards, like painting over a door.
A book of other galaxies, the non-future.
I search for marriages like mine.
Some quietly exist: Hanif and Jane. Callum and Su-Lin.
Lifetimes fold like water, like soft petals.
How something so real can be hidden away.
I think about flow, how archives sweep
the truth until we bring it to light.
You can see it here, the blue line of sadness.

Water of Leith

By the water of Leith you sit & think of the day.
Scrolling down, saw bad news but kept a straight face.
Told yourself: *don't do it, don't give yourself away.*

Your streamlined self exists. Always filtering your words.
Black on black is your staple wear, body conscious.
By the water of Leith you sit by trees: how they bare themselves.

Quiet is a kind of yearning. Those times you loved mutely
as a lover's coat sunk below the hill. If wool was skin
was touch or ache: don't do it, don't give yourself away.

Holding back is an axiom you live by. The other person
speaks first, spiral in their eye, a drop on glass.
By the water of Leith you pull at grass: how easily it tears.

When you look back, there was always a holding back:
No direct maybes, a pull at the mouth's edge
like a zip, gestures that gave nothing away.

It's the way the wind snaps the trees, the way grass bends
to the shore: everything breaks the same.
By the water of Leith you look over the silver edge
folding that thought, over and over, until it folds away.

Playfair steps

At the top, I think: if only you could see me now.
A glance between iron fence poles
framing our wet and gold city. Forward I move

under glutted skies: conflicted, damp
from double rains and I think: Dad,
if only you could see me now. A victory,

like the swinging flags atop the mint building.
Courage is a series of steps. Forward I go
into Edinburgh's old town, past the shadowy

High Court and smoky low-roofed pubs.
If only you could see me now: paler,
curved like a question mark. *I've missed you,*

I'd say. And you'd say, *are you hungry*
and then what? A hug on the corner.
Thoughts like this pierce the day like sirens,

but forward I go through the book-like doors
of the library, to peer at the manuscripts.
If only you could see me now. I see you everywhere:
an image of you sits down in the cafe and I stare.

Brothers

The writer Muriel Spark had an older brother, Phil.
He existed like a tree. In Martin Stannard's biography
of Spark, Phil's big mention is on page twenty,

brief as a twig crunch in the dark. Nobody liked Phil.
Spectacled and short, he flew box kites alone
to decompress from family bullshit. I have no brothers,

only sisters. Growing up I learned to eat fast,
I learned empathy was all in the head tilt, sideways hum.
Muriel Spark's brother had no real impact on her work,

those salty whodunits. He liked typical boy things.
Phil liked to fashion wooden toys and crystal-set radios,
he had the grey drabness of autumn afternoons.

He didn't feel a part of their family, their street like a ribbon
spooling down the hill. He did not feel pink rushes of love
from their parents, Bert and Cissy, who polished

Muriel's halo and left him hanging in the side bar,
his brows mulling future departures.
He wiped his glasses, eyes like sad triangles.

I think about brothers because I have none.
I imagine one; a brother with same determined gaze.
Not sure where I'm going with this; down a hall

into a hospital room, where a priest in aubergine robes
lays his hands on Dad's chest, still as a snowy town.
Our brother Arturo, he kept saying, *our brother now in peace*

but my dad didn't have brothers, he only had us.
That's why I think about brothers so often.
How they exist in all of us, candles in a barn.

Muriel Spark's Mum's Letters

Her scrawl is an insect's path. At first I can't read it.
But then I do! One must think in turns, in dizzy loops.
Y and J appear to be other's reverse.
To understand one's handwriting
you must sympathise with their outer shell:
Muriel, dear. Dearest Muriel,
her mum's voice like a voicemail
you'd listen to while twirling the cord.
A pattern, deliberate as lace:
160 Bruntsfield in the top corner,
as if Muriel would forget where she was born.
Then profuse thank-yous for the money sent home.
Her scrawl is neat as traffic lines
but skitters left when she's upset:
Phil, your brother, is getting meaner!
Problems get brushed under the carpet:
I know you struggled. Nothing else.
Letters float from Edinburgh
to London to New York
back to Scotland's National Library,
their afterlife spent in stamped tins.
I start over, so she speaks to me again.

The Handover

Roadside moss or forest wool: verdant shade of folders.

I look forward most to the handover:
archive's routine dismantling

from submerged box to varied air,
the paper's small indentations
evidence of previous musing.

And it's the handover
invisible ripple
from attendant's hand to mine –
our mutual swapping that inspires my step
on lime and sea foam carpet.

Reading is tiring and endlessly generative.
We sit in collective spaces,
minds spread as aerial photographs.

Out of the box, out of stacks,
from typed case numbers and catalogues
is this life in reverse,
which I take in my hands and hold close.

Frances

You were the only friend Muriel Spark trusted.
Rosslyn House was your shared schoolhouse:
your ribbon colour was apple red.
Don't listen to what Muriel's mum said,
when she ran into you on the street:
She couldn't be bothered to talk to me.
Not true. Your job was to be the best friend of two realities,
you were Jenny in the book, weren't you?
The pretty one, the one the art teacher knelt to kiss.
Your papered voice comes undone in my hands,
yellowed letters falling apart like crushed tulips.
Each February, on Muriel's birthday you sent a floral card.
Never complained, she said of you in her letters.
Your hands waved water lilies during country dancing,
and you vaulted the horse with easy grace in gym class.
This was all in Muriel's last letter to you. I hold it to my face:
scents of peppermints, lavender and time passing.

Dear Frances

My girlhood friend. I'd like to see you again.

Maybe the silhouette
of your ruffled hockey skirt
on the cowslipped, grassy knolls.

I'd like to see the sea cave
where we buried the slips of paper,
the poem we wrote together laid in the sandy bowl.

I'd like to see you,
glittering as a Christmas ornament in Rome,
descending the marble balustrades.

Bless you, old friend,
for never saying how hard it was, when it was.

What makes sense now
are glorified celebrations of fragility,
day's preciousness
reduced to small vapours,
saffron light touching the fences.

Except this: my own silhouette gaining contours
at dusk, when the sky tips light

on the sloped blossomed path,
and dripping willow trees rise

to salty pink sky, and there is light,
there is rain, and you know you've arrived,
less one person.

Are you happy?

The answer is not inside this room, so don't pray
to the ceiling lights. Your friend who asked the question
has an ocean gaze. This is your safe colour.
When you were twelve your room was blue.
Fourth daughter, clever one, looking out.
Now when you look out the window, there's a word –
stratocumulus – for today's crumpled sky.
Your friend takes off her glasses
and you let out enough breath for a week.
It's not the question but how to explain
aspirin's tight taste & blankets over your head.
Words are just sounds we agree to understand.
They don't have to mean anything, can float like paper kites.
You count the lights, panicked. The heart of the room.
What is the heart of the matter?
A candle between you shakes its orange head.
Say I'm happy, I am & this whole scene disappears

Dim Sum Vortex

When you bite into salty egg yolk bun, a co-conscious pairing
of floodlights on still afternoons, of tendrils escaping

when driving too fast; then fried sesame balls
with black seeds of unfurling futures,

before mashed taro topped with candied ginkgo,
lined in vulnerable stratas like married humans,

I catch sight of your mouth. In this dim sum vortex
we sit across from my parents for the first time ever,

triangulating data about the economy, under a sky
crisp as a sugar rose, and you cartograph visible anxiety

sweeping each morsel to mouth. In this tea-stained dive
of Vancouver, against the mountain backdrop

is a kaleidoscope of couples.
I catch sight of your mouth, the way you eat,

the way your mouth forms a question mark.
It's a day in my memory to savour, so that when

people avoid dealing with real life, ask on surveys,
when were you last happy?

I automatically swipe to that day, that day.

No. 18

Our new flat says, here is some brokenness.
There are cracks in the walls and a busted pilot light.
It's not about fixing, but the coming to terms

with sudden winds of ventilators,
casual blooms of flooring mould.
Our new flat tells us that DIY is a waste of

breath. It's all about coming to terms with life,
slick plastering over past hurts,
testing the strength of glue and boards.

Our new flat says, *here's more broken things for you,*
a gash in the door like a wailing mouth,
so you walk by, walk back to soothe the lip.

It's not about fixing, but coming to terms
with the flailing axe against the universe
it's blissful swing sounding so much like agony
that's what it must mean.

Foucault

Foucault, we don't have to be polite anymore.

I think of how you said:
lyricism of marginality finds inspiration in the outlaw

on Princes St, outside the National Gallery,
where the western world shows itself,
all strong pillars and slipped light. I study the art,

sceptical of framed life. Pale bears
more pout: revved-up queens with cello shoulders
cast stink eye to stags on cloud-peaked hills.

Whiteness is a measure of the depth of colour.
Never mind the historical ashen faces,
a harp's gilded curves in snowy parlour rooms,
even the lochs beget a bland glimmer.

All my life I've thought of myself in terms of whiteness,
without realising why.
Everything at its core is white: bones, waves and tofu,

his privately warm chest in our room we rested
behind glass, weren't we just like art,
how our skins blended like two varieties of sand:

a tender bread colour versus a deep terracotta
and how the sunlight framed us.

Foucault, nothing here reminds me of me.
When did it become normal to look
at objects behind glass
and not see yourself? You were right, of course,

to identify with the peripheral: dark barn
misleading the eye, mossy dots cleaving the waterside.
This will be the way into the narrative

until one day, becomes day one.

Cashino

At the junction of stained wall and twice-robbed bank
was the Cashino, apple yellow: lit like an ocean liner,
temple to hacking coughs and day sleepers.

Now it's a place featuring Korean-Scottish fusion:
haggis baos and stovie bibimbaps,
and love blooms in the noodle house.

Were this street a body of water
uni students would form the estuaries
in boyfriend jeans and crop tops, striding in groups of threes.

I've lived here for a while. When people ask me how long
I get vague. Some ghost of me is always in Blackwell's,
pretending to read Kristeva and Lacan,

but it's really the couples I study,
straw haired girls standing with brown-eyed partners
each looking for the look: roll back, to move forward,
the desire to become small, smaller
and sink into the cliffside of one's neck.

It's gone now, the Cashino. Replaced by bubble tea.
I do a double take when I pass where it used to be,

the sign's yellowness more fruit than flower
and how we walked under creamy light,
one of a kind for the first time ever.

Lines

Once upon a line we signed,
our smiles were two upward lines.
Two upward lines like the French doors in the new flat,
our new flat where your drafter's eyes studied lines.
Ice lines in the freezer gone blue from neglect,
and lines on our faces 'cause we overslept.

If a line goes on forever it is a ray; this is a fact.
A fact buried, like frosted leaves on our walk,
our river walk where rays warmed our ears
on Sunday late day, depending on how we felt.

Depending on how we felt we said nothing
when nothing could be an answer,
stood in rooms cut into private spaces,
and crossed cutlery to declare one's hunger.

One day I got sick & the phlebotomist drew lines of blood
blood thinner than the pink sky on the way home,
almost home I stopped at the traffic lights
just as we faced each other eventually
cracked lines in our voices, our voices lines in the dark.

Animals

like lions, we raised our heads on the hill
the winter day we wed at Edinburgh Zoo

like swans we paired for life
like squirrels we saved for the winter glut
like peacocks we dressed in high pomp:
purple streaks above my eyes like tiger stripes,
and your silk tie shimmered like an otter's pelt

like meerkats our guests stood in a half arc
and embraced the noon light, our vows
like parrots we chanted, like elephants we wept
like penguins we nuzzled necks
to the swooping joy of the crowd

like gazelles we raced down a carpet
like rabbits we reached the end and turned round
like monkeys we lifted our palms for rain
you slung your jacket over my shoulders,
it smelled of you completely & fitted like a skin

like honeybees we danced, like hippos we gorged
like pigeons we homed to our sea-facing house
like camels we cast long shadows into the night
and like lions, we lay down

Hôtel Chevillon, Grez-Sur-Loing

Strength, the river. I came each dusk to scribble,
all the writers at the Chevillion did, moody as a family we sat
in the hot clang of summer, imagining ourselves to be kinder,

a shift into drip-fed light. Like the Glasgow Boys who once
unfolded their easels or RL Stevenson crashing through glass
like them, we embraced strength, the river. I ambled over

at dusk, getting over dumb heartaches, balancing a vodka lime
as earth descended into terraces: orchard stilled
in the charred palettes of summer, imagining my work

to be deeper. But I felt hollow. I wrote little. I clocked
Tinder couples on the bridge, their lustful grabs at each other
a kind of strength. The river. I returned around dusk

forever, if we end where we begin. Me and the other writers,
sat distraught as a family, waiting for aliens to land
in the blue stillness of summer, imagining ourselves smarter.

Writers think in this odd, self-deprecating way.
One night a hot air balloon floated across my window
and I pined. What did I want for my work?
Nothing came to mind. Other than: strength, the river.

Fear of future loneliness

Racing by train to see you but there's a fault on the line.
This is why I keep stamps, fold bills in a biscuit tin.
I pop a pill to sleep. Letters fall from my hand.

This is why I press flowers, find the only patch of sunlight
to stand. When you called, I tried to write it all down.
Hurtling by train to see you but there's a fault on the line.

It's not what's said, but the saying. We know the voice
tricks. How words plunge from a cliff as you gulp them.
Sleeping pills taste of mint. Letters folded fall from my hand.

This is why I lay out all my clothes for the morning
& wring wet ones till they're wept out.
Stumbling by train to see you but there's a fault on the line.

This is why I reply to emails fast. Flick coins into fountains
but don't check which wishing side they land.
There's no sleep, even with pills. Letters fall from my hand.

You reach a point when you can see the rest of your life:
a low-level tunnel with rooms to each side
or a nine-car train with decent wifi and a fault on the line.
Take these pills – here. My letters to you fall from my hand.

Kindness

Some kindnesses we'll never know. It's not our fault,
nor is west-bound traffic, nor when baths overflow.
In a gentler world there'd be no rear-view mirrors,

father figures, and empty seats would merely be
vessels scooping light, like the brief glow
of kindness. It won't be our fault

to have wondered, in our mind's secret forest,
whether to have none or three children
or chosen work over love. In a gentler world

there'd be lunchbox notes, fresh mended sleeves,
a hand sweeping your brow for rain that didn't fall,
kindnesses we may never know. It's not our fault

there are train delays, accidents; and night windows
wouldn't reflect the haggard contours of your face,
but the rose blush of other folk's lights.

Before our arms were arms, before we knew our names
before atoms fused with atoms to become cells,
it was decided: some kindnesses we'll never know.
The world is gentle as needles, engines or crows.

Hinterland

You follow your mind to the brink,
knife-glint in the shadow of the Scott monument.
Your face hides your thoughts, your inner life shifts

like trams down the street's conveyor belt,
beyond the clock with the baronial style façade.
Your brows mute your thoughts, your inner life twists

in this city that views the world in arguments.
But not you. You're empty as a stage post-song,
trapping your mind at the brink,

savouring newly wet textures,
the anvil-like castle in its rock bed.
Your eyes veil your thoughts, your inner life stays rich

when silence encloses your words, cleaving a place
for your outer and inner lives to meet.
Your mind races to the brink

in the rippled shadow of the Scott monument,
pretending to be someone else. Your inner life lifts.
This is actually you: the light in left eye's view,
on the other side of the street.

Summerhall

I get lost in white hallways,
struck by framed bodies unfolding
when flashback is a breath, a breath a moment.

I get lost in white hallways,
balance gone in the slow air, art hanging low,
a box tower I mistake for a shadow, an arm.

When flashback is a breath and a breath a moment
colours in the hallway mural
hits you hits you again; this goes on.

I get lost in white hallways,
reading disrupted by elevator bell,
a comforting sound where I thought there'd be none.

When flashback is a breath, a breath a moment,
everything is dream talk: ineffective,
a memory of a boat, of water, altered by my surfacing of it.

It's not breaths we count, but the gaps between breaths,
lost in white hallways,
the stairwell's sharp turn
when flashback is a breath, and the moment, gone.

Carry

The things we carry get washed away.
Stones in the salt marsh, sea leaves on the path.
The longer we hold them, the heavier they weigh

staggering through eel grass to the sunk bay.
Figures work on the dunes, digging up the past
things we once carried. What washes away

is loved again, bronze pins and arrowheads
relaxed in the dirt. We twirl them in the light.
Holding them, how heavy they seem

like the mood in the chapel, facing away
from the jewelled window and south views
of thoughts we once carried. In time

the shoreline will go, the Northumberland coast
is sinking, bearing the bright bones
we find now. How heavy to have been the one

walled in a stone cell by the sea,
telling yourself: *be good, be better.*
Be someone so light all worries wash away:
how heavy, then, the waves must have seemed.

Ordinary life

Ordinary life teaches us that everything returns.
Cutlery to velvet beds, sweaters to cedar chests.
And if we raged against what we can't change

there'd be no denouement, no laying earth
over wood, soil against grain.
Ordinary life teaches us. Everything returns

with a tyrannical sweep: clocks
to the twelfth place, empty fishing boats home.
If we rage. When we rage. Things unchanged

dwell in our bodies, zip through our veins
when you bat the full glass off the edge.
Teach us life is ordinary. Everything returns

half-loved, starved, seeking a den:
salmon to spawning rocks, us to the church gates.
So we rage. Against what is too late:

days that never happened, embraces misspent.
Ordinary life teaches us we must return
to the same front door, same view of bins.
Even the light says, *you were so wrong about this.*

Balmoral Clock

I'm late as usual so I trace the clock like a holy thing.
Study of absolute lines, of light and gold.
Time's arms do not hold us, but point us away

across the gilded bridges, the galleried West end
over Parliament with protestors surrounding
the upturned boat, down to Leith's tumbling coves

and I'm hurrying, late as usual. I scan the
moustache curves of the turrets,
sandstone baronial façade which leads

to the depthless levels of Waverly
and things you want to forget: soft cuffs on their shirt,
welcome slump of their coat on the chair.

My eyes trace the clock's spiky crown
and the window of opportunity that everyone knows,
those extra three minutes it gifts: we all love

time. Enough time for lots of things:
a kiss on the steps, quick text, time to regret
the thing you didn't say, and enough time
to board and look back, backwards as you go on.

White Gloves

Archives, your love is selective. I pull cotton ghosts
over my hands, tip to wrist.
This is what it means to censor
oneself; a vanishing trick,
illusion of cover, no trace of my fingers
on clean acetate. From the envelope I pull
photographs slowly, exorbitantly
with the levelling swoop as if exiting a tunnel.
Strength is what we lose to go forward, from the past.
A series of inter-racial families from two centuries ago.
Their eyes with duty, they gaze at a point
no longer in view: a peach tree
in a flourishing orchard, maybe a wintering boat.
White gloves reduce our touch by allowing us to feel
only mistake; absence of grip, release into the void.
Each person in this reading room holds
a library of voices, exhausted.
I pick and choose, lay them out like cards,
like a rich lady in a sad movie. If that were the case. If only.

Your Paris

'It is a good thing to go to Paris for a few days if you have had a lot of trouble, and that is my advice to everyone except Parisians.'—Muriel Spark

Muriel, I did what you said:
I went to Paris because life sucked.
You know when a grey fog overtakes
and the only cure is lift off.
Here I am in the Tuileries, chasing cola pastries
and ornate pillars of something touristy.
So far I've learned: churches are neutral places to cry,
and Pont Neuf's love locks generate a sick glow.
Thoughts I have, and have again, loop wickedly
like the Arc de Triomphe's roundabout.
So bored I am, in the auberge's whisky light,
restless in the comedown phase of a book party.
My French is so basic the waiters barely nod
and in dive bars I doodle on the toilet wall.
High on gluten, I feel so much love for everyone.
In the metro I make friends with a bandaged dog
and emerge into a radiant vortex
of fibre glass pyramids, where a man
lassoes a twine bracelet round my wrist
Pour vous, he says, *la belle fille*
and because like you, it had been
over four seasons
since I'd been touched — girl, I totally let him.

Muriel's Diaries

For all she displayed, in equal amounts she hid.
Rendezvous in black and social events in red,
a game, in her tender student life, to feel celebrated.

Boxes held the tension of a physical place,
not a window of time, but not only a box,
like the eyes' retinal gaps open, glistening.

She kept one a year, since 1958.
In truly awful colours of spilled coconut and chartreuse.
Not much data in them to suggest the supposed mania,

but I only had the doodles to go on:
sketches of a gladdened castle in rain,
a house with a pathway of trees.

And each year Feb 1, in wispy letters: 'my birthday'
which hurts like a song that makes you sad,
so you reach for it, to hurt again.

Secrets

Consider the secret of secrets,
their ability to sink yet float.
Teetering in us like small, polished cups.
The sacredness of finding yourself alone,
isolating wind, liberated bliss —
Muriel felt that. Wildflowers mapped her walk
down Drury Lane, when she sent out her novels,
her face sanded by rejection slips. And diet pills,
so she was thin, thinner than the soup in her rations booklet.

Not to worry. Her work was a tonic and sustained her.
What she wrote changed the post-war era,
her pockets of prose.
I separate her letters into piles. Cherry-topped
by this letter, when her sadness ravaged an entire winter.
(The kind of thing, you'd think now,
there's help out there. Hotlines for you.
Whatever gets you through the night, do it. Add to cart.)

When she wrote about only eating lettuce,
a slice of tomato and a few crackers,
where was help, when she needed it?
Consider grief a good thing, how it changes the air's electrons.
How there is the change, from the way
when you emerge from a door, into a door,
when the secret is heavy yet light, becomes actual light
and you can't stop thinking about it.

Footnotes comparing Muriel and I

   i) She moved from Edinburgh to London to be a writer.

   ii) I moved from Vancouver to Edinburgh to think.

   iii) She was seen to be running away from her
        responsibilities.

   iv) I travelled the world with one Herschel backpack.

   v) Her parents sent her cards with bouquets.

   vi) My parents sent me dollar store cards with cheques.

   vii) There was the guilt, at Christmas.

   viii) There was the guilt, at Christmas.

   xi) Her doctor's appointments were marked in black.

   x) Dots in my iCal parceled out my days.

   xi) Life of a blackberry starts as white nuts until full bloom.

   xii) Cherry blossoms in the meadows appear in April.

   xiii) Each box in the archive was one year of her life.

   xiv) Each filled bookshelf was one year of my life.

   xv) Her writing embraced human complexity.

   xvi) My poems return to the archived body.

   xvii) Reading archived letters is the difference
        between being a stranger and a friend.

   xviii) Going through an archive you can see
        what is cherished, memorialized and erased.

   xix) Her archive held dresses, diaries, tiny books.

   xx) Last year I just threw everything away.

Muriel Spark's Love Recovery Club

I imagine their hands, but not their faces.
Hands tell a gritty story, fists like bud tulips.
What I called, Muriel's love recovery club,
men who penned disturbing notes and clutched them,
jacket full of coins, to the post box.

Sometimes Muriel replied and sometimes she ghosted them.
Why didn't you answer me, they shouted,
coveting her star sign
and curvaceous signature:
MISS SPARK, you must HELP ME!!!
Those exclamation marks are like shudders, I scribble
as a carnal sunset striped the room.

When the men typed on mint-white paper,
they signed in bold font, a clue to vocal level.
I imagine hand prints; watermarks on book covers.
How some men talk to women is a mystery to me,
beer droplets on their lip, clouding my seashell ear,
giving compliments that boomerang

like one man said to Muriel: *you project
your desires with zest and vigour,*
an internal high five to his own self. I'd seen it before
in a frosted glass, our shoulders like twin violin bows,
but he was only seeing himself, in blue eyed wonder.

A person's love is surprising,
and so is their anger. Triggers in her novels:
barn doors, lace petticoats lifted in attics, leather smells
became mother, wife, loveless house,
girls in pastel sweaters who blanked their jokes.
Their hands, I imagine,

rigid as pitchforks, scoring air
to express hate for the women in her books.

What did you want to achieve, one demanded,
You are a disgrace to literature.
When Muriel declined to reply, she scribbled 'File',
for Penelope, her longtime companion, to look after.

You talk to comfort yourself and that's what they did,
explaining the arc of her novels to her.
How she was different, in a good way.
I should like to shower you with gifts, one said.
It is cold and sunny in New York
and I like Memento Mori very much, wrote another.

I don't know what Muriel thought of the letters.
Maybe she lay them down, sun on tweed sofas,
several cats outside in the long grass.
I imagine her hands, fingertips like pencil erasers
tracing words of men who mistreated her,
of all the men, who mistreated her

folding, folding them away.

Couples Therapy

The solution is to rage at the hourglass on the mantle,
candle of vanilla, ginger spice. To keep your face open,
relax your jaw when your partner tells your marriage story:
We fight. It's our families, they don't get along. It's affecting us –

to the listening room. A room witness to couples dissolving,
aubergine sofa and matching armchair, stone wallpaper
and giant mirror in lieu of a window – metal circle framing
your own eyes, glossy black sadness.

And the therapist you chose off a website for her jazzy glasses
whose voice is deep, like mellow sparks of wood-smoke,
she smiles. *We're here to go on a journey*, she says
or some bullshit, and hands you both tablets

which your partner takes with a sigh, though you accept,
wondering who else has quizzed their own marriages today
in this room built for domestic interrogation. You press down.
The quiz is long, maybe 20 questions.

I am tired of doing all the work in this relationship. *True.*
I find my partner attractive. *True.*
Nduja sausage, corn fritters, view of the canal,
warm white lights on the decking. That was your last date,

you drank hot chocolate and went to bed on your left sides.
We share similar values and have chosen similar paths. *False.*
I easily trust my partner when they're out of the house. *False.*
My partner and I laugh easily with each other. False

Have you finished, the therapist whispers, and you haven't,
but you hate her and your partner too,
for taking their mother's side on Sunday brunches.
So. *I'm leaving*, you say and stand up suddenly

to everyone's dismay and embarrassment,
out of time. You see the hourglass now, bitter brown sand.

Jam

Take solace in the grand vistas of routine.
When you repeat an act every day
it's not habit but addiction.
A 17th-century recipe for jam instructs:
Take raspberries red or white but do not mingle.
Crush with spoon and strain.
If you compartmentalize your grief into small boxes,
life is once again manageable.
Take a breath. Take a sip of pines.
Take a deep dive into your personal shipwreck,
but for only as long as you can stand.
Take the weight of sugar and boil to a candy,
says the recipe written on paper
the colour of streetlights after dusk.
If you compartmentalize days into small jars,
hours are manageable.
Compression is your practice.
You pocket red berries over seaside hills,
tangled wind in your hair.
You stand for some time by the archived books,
some part of you gone
and some part of you still there.

Queen Street Gardens

The year I came most days. Under a silky wind
that guided me to this den, north of the city.
I slid into gardens shaped as a body,

rhododendron bushes round me like dark cloaks.
Enclosed. A dense word,
like the path that takes me round

own my thoughts, past a lady and her dog,
into a clearing of mist, light.
The year my rich friend lent me her key,

otherwise I would not be allowed here,
feeling the disoriented calm after a mistake,
a journey of closeness to smooth green terraces

glistening ruins and half-tolled bells.
This garden reminds me of a body, my own perhaps,
chestnut paths and hilly expanses

and quiet nooks like folded arms. Leaf after leaf,
like screeds kept in the arms of the archive.
The year I came most days, clacked the skeleton key,

saw my spot in the pond's pink light. And I thought:
why does the right decision always make you a little sad?
The year I did slow circles, squared my shoulders
so my body felt mine again. Since for so long, it did not.

Names

A week before we broke up, we had a conversation.
Dhal, garlic naan. Curved notes on the record player.
I think about it, you said. *What we'd name our kids.*
On a copper mug your fingerprints swirled
like the guts of old trees. I agreed: *I think about it.*
Our cedar table grew longer, to accommodate
all the little faces we imagined.
Well, I said. *Leopoldo after my grandpa.*
The only photo of him, in a barong tagalog,
standing on the beach at his sister's wedding.
Leopoldo Felipe. If you like that name.
A conquistador's name, you laughed.
And if it's a girl, you said. *Something from*
my side. Eilidh. Vaila. Callanish.
I wonder what they'd look like, I said.
Eyes like the tender curves of planets.
Mini marionettes of ourselves.
We faced each other and the beam
of goodness is all I remember now,
sitting here, alone at the same table

.

Meghan and Harry move
to Vancouver Island

I know Horth Hill and its network of paths. Rock shelves
blank-faced, like a person hard to trust. Framed by pines,

the press snap them visibly relaxed; digital snow day
of west coast vibes and gore-tex silhouettes.

It's early, misty and our socks bear a fair-isle pattern.
We go up Horth Hill, a monadnock:

stratums of soil, rock and ice packed as cake layers.
We move deer-quiet, thoughts polished to jade,

musing why they're here: to vent, spill tea, shed drama,
storm mushroom trails in uphill spirals,

to be lost. Or to get lost. To climb above cityscapes.
To reach near-summit and see the after

before the before: islands simmering in blue fathoms
of unhappiness. Or hope. And it's this sneak preview

that makes us still, reach out, maybe kiss, maybe look out.
If hikers saw us from a distance they'd wonder

were we rooted to the earth. Thoughts of that kind.
So now we know, this famous couple. They came,

grew armour, turned into trees, and stayed.

Letter from Marie Battle Singer
and James Burns Singer

I imagine them in a still from a movie: Marie at a window
    overlooking Les Halles,
James in a fishing boat in Scotland, above foam and kelp.
    Their correspondence,
while she trained in Paris and he worked on the seas.
    A lemoned letter,
stained by their thumbs, passed between them. She wonders:
    how can I be happy.
When her words are light, her scrawl travels upward,
    footsteps walking out
into the world. Like uphill grass on a mountain,
    both green and white.
They were a famous couple, as things go. Challenging
    the meaning of sound
filtered through language; hers through psychotherapy,
    and his own poems.
I read this letter in a room with large windows.
    My thinking door opens
to all the missed moments we don't see. A letter isn't love.
    Words are not love.
We all end up in the same place. Looking back
    and holding our letters
to the light. Hoping to see the day through.

Last Words of Eliza Junor

So I'm dying. But I'm not unhappy. I'm thinking of you
in this rose bedroom, when yesterday's sun warms the doors.
Time passes in glimpses, in echoes of curlews.
I think in ship knots, tangled memories:
you were not to leave sugar-land, Demerara with us.
I kissed the door in my pinafore. *Never coming back*,
declared William, your son and my brother.
With Father we sailed to Scotland's Black Isle:
land of pines and minke whales, rocks and water.
Nevermind the sun playing keepie-uppies at the stained glass
the day I was baptized. *A private ceremony*,
the priest said; he smiled but I understood.
For school, Father picked dresses for me in colours of sugar:
brown when picked, white when processed, and blue at dawn.
I smoothed the lace: even in cloth, we let light in.
When strangers stared, it was your soft skin they spied.
So much you have missed in your granite bed.
But I have held you in the peaks of my handwriting,
strict teacher's college and London's slums; then back here,
at Rosemarkie's dressmakers. I sewed them in your image.
Your hair in the threads, a faint silver.

Love in a stone

What the new migrants to Stromness must have seen.
This waterfront, like a pop-up book, blurred with the light.
When you face forward, you leave the past behind.
This village is made of stone. Grey houses, sometimes blue,
depending on the time of day. Each day you praise
the smallness of ideas. It's okay for things to be small
and become clearer. Like the tall ships
carrying new families from Hudson's Bay to Orkney.
Indigenous wives, fur trader husbands, swaddled children.
Their faces are fragments within the lines
of letters you read. Some precious things are saved.
A beaver felt hat. Woven snowshoes. An entire world
inside a bead. Stone is a grounding object.
You hold the Labradorite ballast of the ships
sailing the Atlantic. Colours outlast history.
You look up and your daughter runs toward you,
pebbles from the beach in her palm.
And you understand holding on.

Let's be Elizabeth and Marianne

Let's meet outside the library steps. Let's wear bowties
And tweed suits. Let's go to the circus
and not miss it for anything. Let's eat hardboiled eggs,

yolks only. You are right elephants like brown bread.
I'll distract them while you snip hairs
for your bracelet, sun glowing on your wrist.

Let's talk to each other nonstop for thirty-five years. Let's sink
into thoughtful silence. Let's visit your yellow brick flat.
Let's smoke in tiny ashtrays. Let me swipe a nickel

from the subway tray. See how it glows in the light.
Your mother was a teacher. My mother died in an asylum.
Let's take on the roles of people we wish had loved us.

Let's discuss the afterlife. Let's discuss other poets.
Let me wish you were here, playing croquet after breakfast,
watching the World Series. Let's hang pictures of one another

above our desks. Let's send postcards of palm trees
across oceans, until one day you stop sending them.
Let me braid your bracelet of elephant hair,
think of how your face quickly flushed. Until it's not enough.

After the Pamphlet

I'm here in a gloomy Vancouver reading room
looking at how the pamphlet editors wanted to show,
in paper gestures, Filipino migrants in a new city.
They chose Garamond font, ridged like a palm tree.
The headings: *Your Thoughts, Faces of Our Community,*
Future of Our Youth, both underlined and alternating,
like falling Tetris bricks. A sense of travel was hinted
in a mission statement sculpted into a boat, floating p's
like oars over drifts. So much was unsaid but imagined:
homesickness that struck from January to May,
months of soft rain. Sorrow, its trick of spreading,
fills the blank spaces on the righthand side,
white paper rivers and ink blots. Photos like tiles
show the Filipino Christmas party: new families
swinging the pinata, tables of taro cakes and ube rolls.
We save evidence of progress, but not loss;
I close the envelope, with palms like theirs.

Look

I get a certain look from other Filipinas in the city.
Our eyes connect in mutual beam. Curious but kind,
earthy sheen on a cup of coffee. A look that means:
Girl, I get you. Sudden, like the slipturn of summer into dark.
A gaze of edges and curves, like the swirled path through trees.
A look that knows this is home: foam slippers by the door,
nightshade mangoes in red glass bowl. Purple ube cake.
Fried lumpia. Aunties laughing while the TV roars.
This girl wears stripes and cherry lipstick, off-shoulder sweater.
I should say something. Something that we both know:
how was it, bringing your blonde boyfriend home,
reaching over the passenger seat to smooth his collar.
She passes me now, under a line of pink blossoms,
looking the way a deer looks, a wild brown calmness.
A look of constructed peace, that you give the bookshelf
before you fall asleep. One of quiet doubt,
like the gaze you give the traffic lights when you stop.
A look I give then look away. *Hello*, I should say.

Ghost

Tell me how to ghost someone. How to slide into shadows.
In the sloped kirkyard, I circle plots of historical interest.
Crumbled stone. Overlong grass. Ebeneezer Scroggie's remains,

once buried under fog and starlight. Here is the spot
Dickens conjured sugar plums, eyes glinting like money bags.
Three nocturnal visits, like disgruntled ex-boyfriends.

Tell me about ghosting someone. Tell me about ghosts.
Slim. Steamy. Low-tide energy. How to be present but mute.
To be the one not responding to texts, instead doomscrolls

their phone at all hours. How to have no insides,
like a wave. To amble in the sea, like a jellyfish.
To hover with omnipotent knowledge, like a camera.

Tell me how to be a confident ghost. To whistle past
like a bullet train. To be so honest, you're transparent
as a dumpling skin. A ghost made of small grains

that fall through your palm. A ghost of no words
but down bad thoughts. Tell me how to be a seasonal ghost
shimmering red and green above the tinselled tree.
To exist in the realm of what-will-be. To live in peace.

Pointillism

Tell me why your muteness is the ocean folding itself,
gently. The weather is so nice it's depressing,
all drunk sun & empty skies.

Tell me as we lie on striped rectangles
if your limbic system is a network
of choked pathways,
if you imagine the glow of touch before it's given.

Do we both see in pointillism:
dotted sea, surfboards as cut tongues,
wink of coins in water.

Tell me why your face, facing beauty
changes minimally.

Why reach for my hand, squeeze twice and not say.

Tell me if we swam
to the floating dock & hoisted our bodies
onto soaked wood

would our tiny figures live on
in someone else's photo, caught in sway.

Holiday

I know you are gone but dreamed you were on holiday,
to a bucket-list city, one of early summers and low depression,
river flanked by sloped greens and cupcake towers.

A statement of imperialist architecture, you declared.
For the trip you paid a non-refundable sum,
crossed yourself in the lift-off thump. But not gone.

On vacation, where cobbled lanes bloom
into tourist tack. In a café you skimmed a guidebook
overlooking the river, softened by dusk,

view of two men shaking hands, a reconciliation maybe
to which you smiled, sipped a latte crisp with chocolate dust.
You sent a postcard of a pedal boat on a canal, gone.

But not gone. Just in the zone of luxury goods,
towards the cathedral of gargoyles, back to the river
flanked by sloping greens, you lifted a hand

and I awoke. You're gone, I know. The past,
now flanked by sloped greens, brickwork of cupcake towers
your green cap in place, a hand in greeting –
I knew you'd leave eventually, towards the still river.

Purple

This is what the violet at my window knows:
one gust equals one petal gone.

Tiny gap-toothed plant: don't bring yourself down.

Don't think of what you've failed to become.
Think of the purple block

when you close your eyes,
darker than deer heart, lighter than wine.

Think of gushes of missed colour:
a berry's brief life or pool of lilac silk,

plum underside of stones
or the fresh-pressed bruise on your wrist.

If purple is a time, let it be the past
or what the past cannot bring back,

seconds of sky before a storm cracks
or your pulse, those quick and hurtful beats,
the heart's purple repeats.

On Arthur's Seat

how do I lean into nothing: stroll to the grassy edge
and look over without falling

like on train platforms, how near to the yellow line
should people linger

what's the rule for getting close to danger
for things in tight passing: cars buses strangers

how safe are we in rooms of early light
with others we get to know slowly

and how much of our pasts
is too hard to explain

or too tricky, what would happen
if I strode along stamped grass
peered over the edge
into emptiness

trusting myself to the town's tiny lights

Notes

The epigraph is a quote from Susan Howe's *Spontaneous Particulars: The Telepathy of Archives* (New York: New Directions, 2014), p. 24.

Poems about Muriel Spark were inspired by the collection of letters, telegrams and diaries held in the National Library of Scotland. Other poems were inspired by details in *Muriel Spark: The Biography* by Martin Stannard (London: W&N, 2009).

The quote from Muriel Spark accompanying the poem 'Your Paris' is from *A Good Comb: The Sayings of Muriel Spark*, ed. Penelope Jardine (New York: New Directions, 2018), p. 5.

'Registers of Corrected Entries' is inspired by the alternative register of births, deaths and marriages held at the National Records of Scotland.

'Hôtel Chevillon, Grez-Sur-Loing' is inspired by the Hôtel Chevillon Residences for artists and writers.

'Jam' is taken from a 17th-century recipe housed at the National Library of Scotland.

'Letter from Marie Battle Singer and James Burns Singer' is inspired by a letter located at the National Library of Scotland. Marie Battle Singer was the UK's first Black psychoanalyst. Her partner James Burns Singer was a Scottish poet.

The quote from the poem 'Foucault' is from Michel Foucault's book *Discipline and Punish* (1975).

'Last Days of Eliza Junor' is inspired by a letter written by Eliza Junor, a multi-racial woman born in the 1800s. Eliza Junor and her younger brother William left Demerara (now known as Guyana) in June 1816 for the six-week voyage to Scotland. The two were being taken to the Black Isle by their Scottish father and former slave owner, Hugh Junor.

'Let's Be Elizabeth and Marianne' is inspired by details in the book *One Art* by Robert Giraud (London: Pimlico, 1996).

'After the Pamphlet' is inspired by artefacts found in the Peggy Chu Fonds at the University of British Columbia Special Collections.

'Love in a Stone' is inspired by the stories of inter-racial relationships of Indigenous women and Scottish men during the 1800s fur trade. Several families returned home to Orkney during this time. Aspects of the poem are inspired by objects in Stromness Museum and Orkney Library and Archive.

'Ghost' is inspired by Ebenezer Scroggie's grave in the Canongate Kirkyard, which was believed to have been the inspiration for Charles Dickens' *A Christmas Carol* (1843).

'Balmoral Clock' describes the former Great North British Hotel clock. The clock runs three minutes fast daily except on Hogmanay night, in order for citizens to not miss their train.

Acknowledgements

Thank you to the editors of these magazines, journals and anthologies for publishing versions of these poems: *Poetry Review*, *Arc*, *Bad Lilies*, *Magma*, *Under the Radar*, *Umbrellas of Edinburgh*, *Southword*, *Live Canon*, *The Scores*, *Causeway/ Cahbsair*, *Ambit*, *The Dark Horse*, *Wild Court* and *Abridged*.

Thank you to the archivists, librarians and academics at the National Library of Scotland, British Library, National Records of Scotland, Orkney Library, University of Highlands and Islands, Newcastle University's Robinson Library and the University of British Columbia's Rare Books and Special Collections. Special thanks to Colin McIlroy for generous assistance with the Muriel Spark archive. Many thanks to David Alston and Donna Heddle for our illuminating conversations on the history of migrants to Scotland.

I am grateful for the support of an Open Project Grant, Muriel Spark Centenary Award and the Robert Louis Stevenson Fellowship at Hôtel Chevillon in Grez-sur-loing. Thank you to Creative Scotland and the Scottish Book Trust.

Thank you to Linda Anderson for instilling in me a love of archives, for our friendship and for being an early reader of these poems. Thank you to Sinéad Morrissey, Carolyn Forché, Imtiaz Dharker and Colin Waters for reading the manuscript and providing insightful feedback. Thank you to Jennifer Williams and our group of 12 for writerly support. Special thanks to Clare Lees for our insightful chats.

For their friendship and humour, I'm grateful to Allan Radcliffe, George Anderson, Luisa Stucchi, Mary Paulson-Ellis, Pippa Goldschmidt, Jules Knox and Karlissa Hughes. Thank you to those who help make Scotland our home: Laura Stoddart,

Issy McGrath, Gavin McCutcheon, Emma Burns, Jamie Maxwell, Gillian Davidson, Lizanne Henderson, Ted Cowan, John McHugh and Maureen McGregor. Thank you to Anne Duffy for everything. Much love to Pamela Dalziel for years of encouragement and support. I'm grateful to David Lunny and Maureen Baird for giving me beautiful spaces where I could write.

A million thanks to Deryn Rees-Jones for welcoming the manuscript. Your brilliant, kind and patient editing helped me find a path through the poems. Many thanks to Alison Welsby, Sophie McQue and everyone at Pavilion Poetry for their care and expertise in putting the book together.

I'm forever grateful for the support of my parents, Arturo and Helen, my sisters, Dulce, Stella and Lori, and to Paul, Josh, Cole and Roman. Much gratitude to the McGrath family. And to Harry and Sienna, your love means everything to me.